ALBUM OF DOGS

ALBUM OF DOGS

MARGUERITE HENRY

Illustrated by WESLEY DENNIS

ALADDIN

NEW YORK LONDON TORONTO SYDNEY NEW DELHI

Previously titled *Wagging Tails*

ALADDIN

An imprint of Simon & Schuster Children's Publishing Division

1230 Avenue of the Americas, New York, NY 10020

This Aladdin hardcover edition November 2015

Copyright © 1955 by Rand McNally & Company

Previously titled *Wagging Tails*

ALADDIN is a trademark of Simon & Schuster, Inc., and related logo is a registered trademark of Simon & Schuster, Inc.

For information about special discounts for bulk purchases, please contact Simon & Schuster Special Sales at 1-866-506-1949 or business@simonandschuster.com.

The Simon & Schuster Speakers Bureau can bring authors to your live event. For more information or to book an event contact the Simon & Schuster Speakers Bureau at 1-866-248-3049 or visit our website at www.simonspeakers.com.

Jacket designed by Laura Lyn DiSiena

Interior designed by Jacquelynne Hudson

The text of this book was set in Adobe Garamond Pro.

Manufactured in China 0823 SCP

10 9 8 7 6 5 4 3 2

Library of Congress Control Number 55-8890

ISBN 978-1-4814-4257-2 (hc)

ISBN 978-1-4814-4300-5 (eBook)

To Alex

whose tail wags like a metronome

And to Dice

who is clean but not spotless

Contents

CONTENTS

ALBUM OF DOGS

THE SCOT'S COLLIE DOG

BONNIE WAS HER NAME, AND LOVELY AS IT IS IT DID NOT BEGIN to describe the golden glory of her coat or the snow-white ruff that framed her gentle face.

Bonnie's master was a Scotch High-lander, a Mister Peebles, burly and gnarled as the walking staff he carried.

In all of Scotland there was no better man with a Collie. He had trained Bonnie not only to sort and cull sheep but to guide and drive them home alone. All alone.

So well did Bonnie understand her mas-ter and his ways that her mind seemed to dart ahead of his. Why, whenever he fastened his purse

to his belt and she heard the money jingle, her whole being quivered in expectancy. "Another new flock to drive home?" her eyes asked.

One such day the two of them set off in great glee for a neighboring township. There Mister Peebles found a flock that suited him well. Even as he parted with his silver, his face never lost its glow of pleasure.

"Now, gurrl." He turned to Bonnie with a wave of his hand. "Awa' ye go—acrost the moor and home—with the finest flock in the kingdom!"

Bonnie galvanized into action. She rounded up and bunched the flock. She headed them toward the moor, and toward the little fenced-in place high in the hills behind Mister Peebles's cottage.

Mister Peebles, meanwhile, remained comfortably behind, enjoying a glass of grog in the village and boasting that his Collie excelled all others, even as the moon excels the stars.

But late that afternoon, when he returned home expecting to find Bonnie keeping watch over the new flock, he was baffled. Bonnie was not there. Nor were the sheep!

"Hoots, woman!" he exclaimed to his wife. "This be verra, verra strange! Three mile is nae distance for the likes of her. But I'll take me a wee bit of a nap, and first thing ye ken, Bonnie'll be here! And the sheep, too—wagging their stubby tails behind 'em!"

With a grunt of weariness, he lay down on a couch in the kitchen and gave himself up to sleep.

An hour slid by, and another. The moon bulged up over the hills and the sky was dusted with stars when his wife finally shook him awake.

Mister Peebles rubbed his eyes, trying to think back, but his mind was strangely confused. Had he been dreaming? Had he really seen sheep with wool so long? And where was his Bonnie?

Leaping from the couch he ran out into the night, crying, "Bonnie, Bonnie, where are you?" He ran past the empty penfold and, old as he was, he ran on down the hillside, peering this way and that into the darkness. He spied a tatter of mist. Or was it a tumbled cloud? Or moonshadow washing the earth? He squinted into it; he thought he saw it move. Then a lamb blatted, and a ewe baa-aa-ed in reply. Now he knew!

Breathing high and quick, he scrambled back up the hill to the penfold and threw wide the gate. "Gude gur-r-r-l!" He panted out the words as Bonnie herded the flock into the fold. "Gude . . ." His voice suddenly broke in his throat. For there, dangling awkwardly from Bonnie's mouth, was a newborn pup. "Och, Bonnie!" he cried, as a wave of shame rushed over him. "Och, shure I knew ye were going to have little ones. But, Bonnie, m'lass, how could I guess 'twould be this day?"

He took the pup with great gentleness and tucked it into his waistcoat for warmth. Then he stooped down again to praise the mother dog, but she was off, streaking out of sight as he watched.

Three times that night Bonnie returned, carrying another pup and another and another, until all were gathered safe and sound. When at last she settled down to nurse them, Mister Peebles knelt beside her, and brawny as he was, he let the hot tears fall. "Bonnie, gurrrl," he said very gently, "canst ye ever forgive me?" His voice quavered as he stroked the dirt-matted coat. "It aches me to think I made ye drive the sheep whilst ye had little ones to whelp."

Bonnie wriggled into position and looked up at her master with a deep sigh. Why, there was nothing at all to forgive! "It is ye," her honest eyes seemed to say, "that made me a good sheepdog. I durst not for my life leave the flock." Then she licked each of her puppies in turn and, satisfied at last, dropped off to sleep.

The story of Bonnie and Mister Peebles is a true one. And it will probably happen again and again, wherever there are flocks of sheep and Scot's Collie dogs to tend them.

Whence the name "Scot's Collie," you ask? "A moot question," say the Scottish shepherds. They will tell you that for hundreds of years they raised black-faced sheep known as "colley sheep," and the faithful dogs who tended them were called "Scot's colley dogs."

The English, on the other hand, also lay claim to the name. In old England the word *colley* meant "the black soot off the kettle." And since the original Collies were black as soot, the name may have sprung from this very old meaning.

But whatever and wherever the source, the Collie is known the world over as a steadfast shepherd. In all weather—in snow's blinding fury, in sun's burning rays—he goes about his business, policing the sheep, rounding up the strays, guarding the flock. He will even fight his own relative, the wolf, to protect the sheep. Not that he loves the sheep so much, but that he loves his master more.

THE MERRY BEAGLE

He's small enough for the house, and big enough to be the best rabbit hound that ever lived. Rabbits are his dish. Not that he's a killer at heart. He's a sportsman! It's the thrill of the chase that gives zest and purpose to his life. Whenever he's hot on the trail, his happiness grows so big within him that he sings out in a melody that ripples and rings across the fields. "Music Maker of the Meadows"—that's what he's called!

He hunts pheasant and squirrel, too, but rabbits are his specialty. Their scent is delicate, their ways cunning, but he can unravel the trickiest trails and can make turns and doublings as quick as any one of them.

Way back in the time of King Arthur this small flop-eared fellow was already a work hound, tracking hares for the King and his knights. Years later, when Elizabeth I was Queen of England, she tried to improve the Beagle. She had him bred littler and littler until she could carry one around in a glove. The squires of her day would fill their saddlebags with these miniature hounds and then turn them loose on the heath to go a-hunting.

What a ridiculous failure it was! The work of the Beagle became miniature too, and his bell-toned voice smalled down to a quaver.

Fortunately this fad of the glove Beagle wore itself out. Today's hound measures a full thirteen to fifteen inches. He's still a smallish fellow compared to Setters and Pointers, but he's so brawny and well-muscled that he is a lot of hound for his inches.

The name "Beagle" comes from the French *beigle*, meaning "small." While the French thus named him, it was the English who made him popular. Beagling was, and is, one of their favorite sports, and we in America are fast adopting it.

What is beagling? Is it hiking to hounds? Of course it is. But, oh, how much more!

Picture in your mind's eye a meadow wide open—the earth wet, the breeze gentle. Suddenly a cyclone of Beagles bursts onto the field.

Noses busy, tails merry, ears flying, they are puzzling out a rabbit trail. And puffing in pursuit come the beaglers themselves—men afoot, wearing green coats and white breeches. One among them sights Molly Cottontail and lifts his horn to blow, "Tally-ho! Tally-ho!"

Almost at the same instant the whole pack of hounds catches the scent. In full cry they are on the line, circling the rabbit, driving her ever inward to the beaglers. But by some miracle of speed and timing she slithers her way out of the pack to the meadow's end, and there in a tangle of brake and bramble she dives into her hole.

Does it matter to hounds and men that Molly Cottontail has escaped? Not really. Sporting beaglers are secretly glad when she is driven safe into her nest to run again another day.

In beagling it is teamwork that is all important. But, aside from this highly organized sport, there is always the lone Beagle and the lone boy who were made one for the other. They hunt or hike, just the two of them, shar-ing the good smells of the woods and fields, in tune with the whole wide world.

The Gentleman Boxer

RUDY DOCKY, A FAST-TUMBLING CLOWN FROM AUSTRIA, knows Boxers as well as he knows the sawdust ring. He believes that Boxers and circuses, and boys and girls belong together. He trained a whole troupe of Boxers to play a rough-and-tumble game of basketball. Always the game was such fun for the dogs that the children in the audience jumped up and down in glee.

First, Rudy clumps on stage, his big shoes flapping like a beaver's tail. Then he blows a shrill note on his whistle, and from both wings the dogs come racing out, five to a side.

As Rudy tosses a balloon into the air, bedlam breaks loose. They all jump for it, and the game is on! Playing with head, forepaws, and snub noses, they bunt and bat and shoot.

But wait! There's a foul! One fellow, hugging the balloon tight, pricks it with his toenails. And *pffssst*—it bursts!

Quick, Rudy, a new balloon!

Again the players get set. Again the whistle. Again the game is in full swing—players blocking, passing, dribbling, until the whole stage is churning with dogs. Rudy shouts: "Stick to him, Rex! Don't double-dribble! Pass, Buster, pass!"

At last one leaping fellow shoots a basket, and whether it was his own basket or not, the game is won. Any leftover balloons are now tossed onstage to be kicked and pricked for the sheer fun of it.

And so, with children shrilling in delight and dogs dancing on their hind legs, the act is over.

Boxers are born ball players, says Rudy. In fact, they use their front paws the way a human fighter uses his fists. Some say that's how the Boxer got his name.

He is a fighter, too—a lusty, gusty, hard-biting battler—but only when there is a real need to fight. He seems to know when to fight and when not to. In his native Germany this reasoning power won him the title of "The Gentleman Boxer."

His ancestors were the mighty Mastiffs who grappled lions and leopards, bears and bulls, and held on with teeth locked until the hunters arrived. From these Mastiffs, crossed with large Bulldogs, came the Boxer we know.

Big and strong as he is, there's a gentle side to his nature, too. Youngsters can pull his ears and poke his ribs, and he takes it all with gay good humor. As pet and protector, he is full of love and faithfulness for everyone in the household.

To look at, he is a square sort of fellow, square of muzzle and square of stance, with a glossy coat of fawn or brindle. The black mask on his face is his trademark, and the blacker it is, the better. The deep furrows between his eyes make him look sad because he can't look anything else.

But, remember, he is not really sad. On the contrary, Rudy says, he is full of pranks. Often a rascally fellow will bite the balloon just to see Rudy run for another. And if the basketball game is not exciting enough, one player jumps into the audience, upsets the hot-dog vendor, and shares the loot with his pals.

The Misunderstood Poodle

H E IS IN LOVE WITH LIFE, BUT THE MOST MISUNDERSTOOD dog in the world. He is strong enough to fight through bulrushes with a flapping duck in his mouth, or to take hurdles that would do credit to a horse. In intelligence he ranks as one of the smartest. Yet the world thinks of him as a dude and a dandy, a bauble of curls and wool.

How can we show you that he is a vigorous fellow in spite of the rosettes on his hips, the bracelets on his legs, and the bangles and bows in his pompadour?

First, let's skip across the centuries to the days when he was used as a bird dog. He was such an enthusiastic retriever that he would swim about for hours to find a maimed duck. To speed his progress through the water, the hunters sheared the heavy wool from his hindquarters. He did swim faster as a result, but the owners now began to worry. Were not dogs subject to rheumatism just like people? Should not their joints be kept warm? And so they devised the Poodle cut—leaving a pompom of wool on hips and hocks. As for the tuft on the tip of the tail, this became a direction flag, signaling the dog's whereabouts.

For two reasons this custom of clipping has come down the centuries. At dog shows it is easier for judges to study bone structure if the body is not hidden by blankets of wool.  Secondly, unlike other dogs, a Poodle does not shed his hair. It grows long, like human hair. But instead of growing lank and loose, it twists into heavy, ropelike curls. The weight of such a coat would be enough to change a blithe spirit into a rag rug!

The joy of living is in the blood of the Poodle. Whatever role he plays, he throws his whole heart into it. Acting is pie to him. At age two months he is ready to follow his mother onstage as a tumbler. And before he is a year old, he can manage more serious roles. You may have seen the Poodle Coco in the circus. Dressed in starched cap and apron, she pushes a carriage full of pups into the spotlight as deftly as any nursemaid. Or have you seen Mimi high-dive into a swimming pool and then float around on a rubber raft like any bathing beauty?

Other Poodle performers turn somersaults, both front and back, jump over kegs on their hind feet, skip rope, trundle toy wheelbarrows, and even spell out words with children's blocks.

The Poodle is, and always has been, actor and friend to royalty. When Queen Anne of England grew weary of her duties, she called for a troupe of Poodles known as "The Little Ball of Dogs." Forgetting her cares, she would laugh and clap her jeweled fingers as they danced prettily to music. And when they put on a spirited battle, firing guns with their forepaws, the Queen rose to her feet and cried, "Huzzah!"

Today, Poodles come in three sizes—standard, miniature, and toy. And they come in solid colors—black, white, silver gray, apricot, and brown. Their uses are many, for their quickness to learn fits them for the circus ring, the hunting field, or the drawing room. Poodles are *people*, one owner insists, enchanting people! Their sparkling eyes look out upon life with wisdom and gaiety.

OLD SOUR MUG, THE BULLDOG

A S IS TRUE WITH PEOPLE, THE UGLIEST DOGS ARE OFTEN the most gentle. Old Sour Mug is a loving soul. He likes nothing better than to lumber up on his master's lap— all sixty pounds of him—nuzzle his massive head under a protective arm, and snuff and snort in a kind of ecstasy.

Yet this overgrown lap dog will fight to the death if necessary. He seems almost insensible to pain.

Why is this? How can it be? Perhaps because once upon a time he was a fierce and fearless bull fighter. He knew only one life, and it was fraught with danger and with pain.

In Old England, for seven hundred years, his ancestors provided a strange kind of sport known as bull-baiting. At a marketplace or some so-called garden, men roped off an arena. And within it they neck-chained a maddened bull to a stake. The chain was long enough to give the bull complete freedom of the pit, but short enough to protect the milling mob that packed itself about the ring.

At the appointed hour the fight begins. Into the pit men toss a quivering dog. He is drawn to the bull, the way a piece of steel is drawn to a magnet. His low-slung body shuffles along, a small shape inching forward to death or victory.

A moment of stillness. Then with a bellow the big bull comes charging across the pit, head down, sharp horns ready to gore.

The dog stands his ground. Then suddenly, with a quick upthrust of his jaw, he reaches for the bull's nose. He has it and he holds it!

In a mad frenzy the bull wheels and runs, jerking his head violently, shaking the dog's body like a whip. But he cannot shake free. He tries slapping the dog against the stake, then buffeting him around and around the arena, but the pinning hold on his nose only tightens.

Minutes drag. The pit is a swirl of dust and fury. At last the bull can stand the pain no longer. With the crowd roaring and howling at him, he sinks exhausted to the earth.

For this savage sport of "pinning the bull" men developed a special breed—a Bulldog. His body had to be low to the ground so that it would not be a target for death-dealing horns. And his nose had to be flat so that he could breathe with his face up against a bull's.

Dramatic and exciting as the sport was, it could not last. Men began to feel ashamed at matching a small dog against a big bull forty times its weight. Even though the dogs were not often killed, the pain they endured was too cruel.

And so, in 1835, the "butcherly" sport was ended by law. But dog-lovers did not let the Bulldog die out for want of a job to do. They bred the gentlest to the gentlest until they developed the mildest dog in the kingdom.

The Bulldog is still the symbol of British tenacity. Yet today he is the children's pet—a wrinkled, endearing fellow with a toothy smile and a great, gentle heart.

The Cocking Spaniel

IN DAYS LONG GONE BY, THE DIMINUTIVE LITTLE COCKER with the big soulful eyes was a gun dog. By instinct he was a hunter, and by training he became an expert.

In England, where woodcock abounded, he would thrash into the thickest brush to rout a cock from its hideaway. Often he emerged scratched and bleeding, but his stump of a tail wagged happily. Had he not flushed the woodcock into the air? Had not his master shot it?

"All right then!" his dark eyes said as he delivered the fallen bird into his master's hands. "Let's do it again!"

And with the same eager, bustling happiness he plunged into the thicket again, unmindful of the thorns and cockleburs that latched onto his long, floppy ears.

Because this tireless little hunter was such an expert on wood-cock he became known as a Cocking Spaniel. The "Spaniel" part of his name came from Spain, the country of his birth.

When the Cocker was introduced into America, a curious thing happened to him. Over in England his pleasing appearance had been taken for granted. But here in America children, and grownups, too, found him irresistible. They liked his silky coat and his handy size, but what really intrigued them was that he looked so sad and glad all at the same time! His face wore a mournful expression, yet his tail was perpetually merry. Americans everywhere took him right out of the fields and into their homes.

Pixie, a wavy-coated blonde, became a typical Cocker pet who never worked the fields at all. As a roly-poly pup she had been full of mischief—chewing new and old slippers, sneak-ing candies off the table, tipping over waste-baskets and garbage cans.

Knowing how sensitive she was, the family decided to punish her exactly as they punished their own children. In a corner of the liv-ing room between soft, comfortable chairs stood an antique one with a hard scoop seat. After each offense Pixie was made to sit on the chair, like any naughty child.

Of course she hated the "Naughty Chair." It made her feel such an outsider! Life went on all about her, the children romping and playing without so much as a look in her direction. Always, as the minutes wore on, the scoop seat grew harder and harder and she grew lonelier and lonelier until life became unbearable.

Never did a wrongdoer learn more quickly! In a matter of weeks she outgrew her puppy tricks until the Naughty Chair was seldom used. Eventually she ignored it completely, sauntering by, high-nosed, as if it did not exist.

But in the far recesses of her mind Pixie never really forgot. On the day when she found her puppy chewing on a red satin slipper, she could not resist the fun. Dancing around him in dizzy delight, she snatched the slipper away and gave it a fierce shake to show him just how it should be done. Then, heartily ashamed of her crime, she leaped up onto the Naughty Chair to take the punishment for them both!

THE GERMAN SHEPHERD

ALWAYS THE GERMAN SHEPHERD HAS LIVED IN A KIND OF dog heaven. On the boundless sheep ranges of Germany his career began—herding sheep, driving them, guarding them with his life. Yes, he knew footsoreness and weariness, and he had to fight wolves and wind and storm. But wasn't his master right there, commanding him, praising him for work well done? And at the tag end of day, when the flock was all bedded down for the night, didn't his master share black bread and cheese with him? And didn't they, side by side, hug the fire and watch the moon come up?

Life was all good for the German Shepherd—the work, the sameness of his days, and, over and above everything, the ecstasy of sharing earth and sky with his master.

Then Time changed the face of Germany. Steam trains came

whistling across the ranges, carrying livestock to market. They made sheep driving unnecessary. And settlers began pushing outward from the cities, shoving the sheep farms back into the hinterlands. With the years the farms became smaller and smaller, until finally they were boxed in by fences. Now there was no need for protecting the sheep, and so no need for the shepherd dog!

The breed might have petered out if the German police force had not foreseen a new role for this big fellow. They trained him to attack criminals with the same ferocity he had once attacked wolves. And soon the whole world knew of him, not as a shepherd but as a police dog.

Then war came. World War I it was called. The new police dog 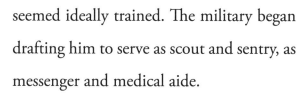 seemed ideally trained. The military began drafting him to serve as scout and sentry, as messenger and medical aide.

But it remained for the blinded men left over from war to raise the police dog to his full glory. Once again he became a shepherd—leading, guiding, protecting.

Today, in a half dozen countries, thousands of German Shepherds are going to

Seeing-Eye schools. They are such bright and eager pupils that in a matter of months they learn to signal down-curbs by sitting down and up-curbs by stopping. More important, they are capable of fine reasoning. While *they* can walk under a scaffold or a low awning, they learn to swing clear of it for their blind masters.

You yourself may know one of these dog graduates. You may have watched him striding along at an even, machine-like pace as he leads a blind person through the snarls of city traffic.

But the great miracle of the Shepherd's work is his aloofness to dog temptations—to tantalizing meat and gravy smells wafting out of restaurants, to cats streaking across his path or spitting in his face, even to the come-play-with-me bark of some friendly mongrel. These distractions seem unworthy of his notice. He actually prefers the companionship of his sightless master! Heads up, eyes forward, they go marching along together, a man-dog team held close not by harness and handle, but by love.

Once again the German Shepherd has found his dog heaven.

LITTLE LION OF PEKING

THE PEKINGESE IS A PARADOX. HE LOOKS LIKE A MORSEL OF fluff, but lift him up and you find him surprisingly heavy. He is built like a lion, massive in front with an enormous shaggy mane. And he is lion-hearted, too. I knew of one who defied even a Great Dane. He would bring out his playthings—his rubber bones and tinklebells—and taking a war-like stance, forefeet wide apart, he would roar in the big fellow's face.

Luckily the Great Dane always loped off in disgust. But "little lion" was supremely happy, believing his fierceness had frightened the big dog away.

In the heart of the household, however, the Pekingese is all play and gentleness, more kitten than lion. Fastidiously he washes his face and paws after eating, and he picks his way among fine bric-a-brac nimbly as a cat.

Perhaps he is at home with fine things because his ancestors lived among porcelain and jade, teakwood and carved crystal. They were the palace dogs of China, the pampered pets of emperors and empresses, and they lived in great splendor and luxury.

"Is not Buddha our teacher?" the high priests said. "Is not the lion his protector? Therefore we hold the little lion dog sacred and guard him with our lives."

Emperor T'ai Tsung thought so much of the tiny dogs as religious symbols that he used four of them as his escorts. Bamboo Leaf and Plum Flower strutted ahead of him, heralding his arrival with short barks. Pomegranate and Precious followed in his wake, bearing the hem of the royal robe in their teeth. The people made way and bowed in reverence to emperor and dogs alike.

Empress Tzu Hsi was moved to write a poem about the lion dog, and, strangely enough, today's standard for the Pekingese is taken from her description.

"Let the lion dog be small," she wrote. *"Let it wear the mane of dignity around its neck. Let the tail billow over its back. Let the muzzle be black and appear to be sliced with a knife downward from the forehead.*

"Let its eyes pop and its ears be set like the sails of a war junk.

"For its color let it be that of the lion, a golden yellow; or let it be red or sable or apricot, or striped like a dragon, so that there may be dogs appropriate to each of the Imperial robes."

The Empress ended her poem by prescribing a wondrous diet:

"Let his meat be the breast of quail and sharks' fins and curlew livers. And let his drink be tea brewed from peach buds, and broth from the nests of sea swallows."

For centuries the little lion dog thrived in the seclusion of the Imperial Court. Then in 1860, near the close of the Chinese war, English troops entered Peking and looted the palace. They found five little dogs waddling forlornly about the deserted courtyard. To the English captain they seemed like exquisite pocket charms to take home as mementos.

It was these little refugees that founded a new breed in the Western world. And so popular has it become that the Peke is now the toy dog of the day, lionized by all who admire great courage and quiet dignity in one so small.

THE SPOTTED DOG OF DALMATIA

ONCE THERE WAS A MOTHER DOG NAMED POLKA DOT. Each year her owners went off on a summer's holiday to England. The leave-taking at the boarding kennel was both sad and brave. The dog did not whimper. Nor did the two boys cry. Solemnly they each placed in her cage one of their old tennis shoes for memory's sake. Then, wordlessly and without a backward glance, they walked away.

But one year the family could not bring themselves to leave Polka Dot at a kennel. She was about to have puppies, and they wanted her to be in a home as nearly like theirs as possible. Besides kindhearted parents, there had to be two children at least, and there *had* to be horses! For Polka Dot was a Dalmatian, a coach dog, and everyone knows Dalmatians like horses the way bees like flowers.

Polka Dot's summer home turned out to be a happy refuge. Wesley Dennis was chosen to care for her, not only because he is a dog's kind of man but because he has two boys and six horses!

In her new surroundings Polka Dot found complete happiness. She soon gave birth to her puppies—eight chubby ones—right in Wesley's studio. To his amazement, but not to hers, they were pure white with no indication of the black spots to come!

The summer days lazied themselves away. Through the open windows Polka Dot breathed in the good smell of the horses, and she brought up her puppies to like it, too.

Then one day came word from England: "When Dot's puppies are weaned, you can give them away." Sorrowfully Wesley gave his best friends their choice until only one pup was left. Suddenly he realized how empty and lonely the studio would be without a pup tearing his paint rags or sleeping at his feet. "I'll keep the last one myself!" he decided. "And I'll name him Dice."

And so, when Polka Dot went back home to her people, little Dice was left as a keepsake.

By show standards Dice is not a good Dalmatian. His spots run together. "But he wouldn't like dog shows anyway," shrugs Wesley, "and neither do I. His love is horses. The big thing in his day is the canter we take every morning. He is so afraid I will go off without him that, right after breakfast, he starts sitting by my boots. If I'm delayed, he goes to sleep on top of them.

"Riding with him is fun," Wesley says. "He doesn't get under the horse's feet at a full gallop or run way ahead and chase sheep, as my other dogs did.

"We are never far apart, if it can be avoided. When I went to the Grand Canyon on the Brighty story, I missed him so much I used to send him bones by parcel post.

"One thing is strange about Dice. He can't stand anything wet, even a drop of water. It is funny to see him try to cross a brook without getting his feet wet. And when it's raining, he tries to run *under* the rain. He's had only two baths in eight years. He suffered so much, I just gave them up.

"Even so," laughs Wesley with a wink at Dice, "he always looks clean, though I can't say he's spotless!"

Fox Terrier—Dog with a Past

WE WERE STANDING ON THE BUSIEST CORNER IN Cleveland, a mounted policeman and I. Traffic screeched to a noisy stop, and moved on as the lights changed from red to green. People bunched up at the curb, then swarmed across the intersection. Horns shrilled. Motors roared and coughed up fumes which mingled with the haze of city smoke.

Yet, here, in all the noise and bustle a drama was taking place. A gay little Fox Terrier, was reaching up to touch noses with an obviously delighted horse. The two creatures were of one world and one mind, and for them this other world of busyness did not exist.

"What are they saying?" I asked Tony, the cop, for there were definite little snortings on the part of both.

"At first I couldn't tell either," admitted Tony, "but now I understand."

"You understand what?"

"What they say, of course."

"But what *do* they say?"

The policeman hesitated. He had one eye on traffic, one on the little scene before him. "Each day it's different. Sometimes it's just pleasantries. But you . . ." He smiled in embarrassment. "You wouldn't understand."

"Try me."

"All right. But if you doubt or laugh, I don't go on."

"Hmmm," I nodded. And that was the last sound I uttered until he finished.

"Pete is a city dog. Sure, I know lots of Fox Terriers are city dogs. But Pete is a downtown dog. Never saw a tree. It's like living in a canyon, the way he lives—a canyon of stone buildings. Think of it! No trees! Not even a bush or a blade of grass. Plenty of fireplugs, concrete sidewalks, but no trees!

"My horse, Skippy here, is his only link with the green world outside. Skippy seems to give him all that he misses. When Skippy talks, his breath is sweet with hay and clover. And what he says is full of danger, excitement, and adventure. Why, the day after the circus fire, when Skippy rescued nineteen horses, he told Pete all about it. How do I know? Well, first Pete smelled Skippy's burned forelock and said, 'What's this strange smell I smell?'

"And then I swear Skippy told him the whole story. Else why did Pete begin to lick the burned places on Skippy's neck, and why did he whine and whimper and make over him exactly like he was a hero? Which he was!

"Pete feels as if Skippy here is a link to his past. Over in England, Fox Terriers knew danger and excitement too. They traveled with horses and hounds, tracking the fox to his den and then bolting him out of it. That's why they were bred.

"But Pete? Why, he'll never even snuff a fox. Mice is the best he can do. He's city-bred and like as not will live out his days in that swell hotel over yonder. No trees. No grass. Not even a shrub."

The policeman sighed. "But look at him. He's happy, living part of his life by proxy, the way some folks live through the books they read. It's just lucky for him that he found Skippy, a horse that can talk!"

The Pointing Dogs

AT THE FIRST BREATH OF AUTUMN, WHEN A BLUE FOG throws a halo over the landscape, a stirring feeling gets into the heart of bird dogs. If their masters do not come for them, they pace restlessly up and down their kennel runs, and at night their sleep is broken by dreams. But their masters nearly always do come, for they, too, are stirred by the same urgency to taste the autumn air and to range over exciting game country.

All dogs have the hunting instinct. But in some it reaches a transcendency. In the big-limbed Pointer, hunting is the stuff and purpose of his life. Should his master fail him, he often breaks free of high wire fences and hunts on his own. So great is his need.

How well and how simply he is named! *La punta*, in Spanish—"The Point."

Did he come originally from Spain, this bird-finding fellow? Perhaps yes. Perhaps no. But in England he was perfected. When first we hear of him, he was a slow-going, rather awkward hunter with an irritable, even a fierce, disposition. But English fanciers bred him to Foxhounds, and then he worked faster and surer. Later they crossed his blood with Setter blood, and then his disposition sweetened.

One Englishman, Sam Price by name, bent all his efforts to create a Pointer with a nose so quick and sensitive that he would have to gallop across fields in order to keep up with it!

By some miracle he produced Champion Bang. Bang had everything. Nose, and speed, and joy of working. He quartered a field like a zigzag of lightning. And when he came upon his birds, he froze in his tracks, hypnotized by the scent. His tail went rigid and his whole body pointed as if a tight thread were stretched from his nose to the bevy of birds. He was invincible, and he worked with Sam Price as an equal, not as dog and master.

When Bang's son, Bang-Bang, arrived in America, he set the style for a dog who loved to hunt, even better than he loved his master.

Is the Pointer the only dog who has learned the art of saying: "Here they are, partner . . . come and get them"?

On the contrary, there are three Setters—the English, the Irish, and the Scotch—who also point their game. They all have the same heritage and the same desire to hunt. Yet how different they are!

Strangely, it is the English Setter and the Pointer who are more nearly alike. Both are white-bodied and both are freckled—sometimes with black, sometimes with liver or lemon. Against the russet tones of autumn their white coats stand out sharply.

But, more important, they are both intensely competitive in spirit. In Field Trials each one has a burning desire to be first to find partridge or quail or woodcock. Each one wants to find the birds faster than the dog he is matched against.

IRISH

SCOTCH

ENGLISH

For years the short-haired Pointer and the long-haired English Setter have been the two pointing dogs most eager to win. Even their puppies, entered in the "Nursery Stakes" of Field Trials, show a lively competitive spirit. Of course, sometimes they are scatterbrained and chase bumblebees or swallows instead of game birds, but all is forgiven in the Nursery Stakes.

What of the Irish Red Setter? And what of the Scotch Black-and-Tan Gordon? Are they not competitors at the big trials? In all honesty, no. Perhaps one day soon they will step out and challenge their English cousins to a win, but meanwhile they are more petted at home than praised afield.

The beauty of the Red Setter has almost been his undoing as a hunter. That rich

mahogany coat became such a temptation to Show Dog fanciers that they kept breeding for color instead of for bird sense. Of course, they could not breed out the hunting instinct entirely, but today's Irish Setter is happier to place his head on his master's knee than to thrash through brush and brier after bird scent. The hunter himself is quite willing to leave his loving Irishman at home, for when the landscape is all red and gold with autumn, a careless friend might shoot the dog because of his invisibility.

Like the Red Setter, the Black-and-Tan Gordon is also color-handicapped. He seems part of the landscape, especially at dusk when hunting is at its best. Then his black and tan color melts into burned-over tree stumps and dense cover.

All three of the Setters are descended from the famed Setting Spaniels who, in days long ago, crouched, or "set," as they neared a covey of birds. The fowler would then throw a huge net over the birds and the dogs both, and so gather them all in.

But with the invention of firearms the net was discarded, and the dogs were taught to stand on point instead of to crouch. This was a simple step in training, for a dog naturally stops a moment before springing his game.

There is magnificence in the restraint of the pointing dog. Eagerly, hour after hour, he hunts his heart out, but when he finds the birds he stiffens into a direction flag. Rightfully, those birds are his. If he were a child, he might scream: "They're mine! Mine! Let me at 'em!" Instead, he suppresses his natural instincts and gives the glory to his master.

Of all pointing breeds the speedy Pointer is generally conceded to be the best bird finder. Why, then, does anyone choose a Setter?

One reason may well be that the Setter loves the master for himself, while the Pointer likes any man with a gun.

Then, too, not every hunter insists upon a wide-ranging fellow. Some prefer a dog who works in close and looks often to the master for help and direction. The bold, swashbuckling Pointer is fine if it's a big bag of birds you're after, but if you prefer that look in the eye that speaks of eternal devotion, then a Setter is the happy answer.

So there you have them—the long-haired English, Irish, and Scotch Setters, and the short-haired Pointer. Good, honest, game dogs all, and yours for the choosing.

SPEAKING AS A SPRINGER

DEAR READER: *I'd like to set paw to paper and do my own chapter in my own way. I am a Springer Spaniel, white with black tickings. Tickings are little splashes of color, as if someone had shaken his fountain pen all over you.*

"Baldwin of Lockridge" is my kennel name. But The Gunner (he's my boss) calls me "Boy." He calls me other things too. Whenever he asks me to teach a puppy how to spring a rabbit or flush a bird, then he calls me "The Professor." I'd rather not be The Professor. Please don't misunderstand. I like puppies. But they puzzle me! When the air is delicious with the smell of pheasant, how can they possibly stalk a butterfly? How can they do it?

Me? I just live to hunt! Give me a crisp day, and The Gunner at my heels, and I'm in my glory. There's one hunt I'll never forget.

I can still see everything, right from the start. The Gunner puts me down in a cornfield and says, "Spring 'em out, Boy!"

It was a world of smell. Hardly had I sampled the air before I knew we'd found birds. With a rush I was on the scent, my tail wagging to The Gunner to come along.

Everything happened fast. The birds were there all right, a big covey of

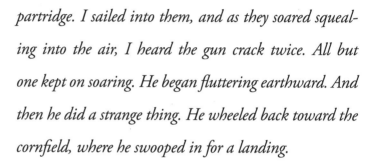

partridge. I sailed into them, and as they soared squealing into the air, I heard the gun crack twice. All but one kept on soaring. He began fluttering earthward. And then he did a strange thing. He wheeled back toward the cornfield, where he swooped in for a landing.

I marked the spot, raced toward it, but when I got there I saw nothing but the dust he was raising. What a runner he was! Only the tip of his wing had been hit and he could go like the wind. He dived now, down the corn rows, then doubled back again. I sprinted after him, twisting and turning until I was dizzy.

In the distance I could hear The Gunner calling me in. There was disgust in his voice. But I couldn't go back now!

The partridge was trying to trick me. I had to outwit him! I circled far around, and when he came plummeting head-on toward me, I jumped him and grabbed his plump body with my teeth. Then in triumph I fetched him back to the hands of The Gunner.

Well, you should've heard him! He laughed like a brook, and the pride in his voice made me wag from stem to stern.

"Boy," he said huskily, "you've got character! You had to be disobedient to me or to your job, and you made the right choice. If every gunner had a dog like you, fewer birds would be wasted."

This story makes me out a hero, but in all honesty I have my limitations. First, I cannot take the place of a Pointer or a Setter because I don't point my birds. I spring them.

Second, I am not as great a retriever in icy waters as, say, the Labrador. I just haven't his coat. Or his size.

What I always do when I meet a Pointer or a Retriever is walk right up to him, give his nose a poke and a sniff, and say, "All right! Suppose you can do your particular job better than I can. I'm an all-around bird dog. I find, flush, and retrieve. I can give The Gunner as much good hunting as two or three specialists! That's me, fellow. A lot of dog in one."

Honestly yours,

BALDWIN OF LOCKRIDGE

P.S. Only one thing I refuse to do, and that is to be a watchdog. I just can't bark at burglars. I like them! Even burglars have some good in them. Well, I just like people—that's all.

The Labrador, King of Retrievers

ON THE FAR-OFF ISLAND OF NEWFOUNDLAND THERE WAS once a big breed of black dogs used as fishermen's helpers. They swam from ship to shore, dragging nets of cod and salmon, herring and lobster.

"St. John's Water Dogs" they were called, after St. John's, the capital of Newfoundland. But the name did not hold—all because of an Englishman, the Earl of Malmesbury. He liked to watch the ships from Newfoundland unloading their cargo at Poole Harbor, England. But it was not the cargo that fascinated him; it was the fishermen's dogs! They could retrieve anything, in any kind of water, in any weather.

The Earl had been wanting just such help. His own brace of Spaniels were fine at flushing a bird into the air, but when it fell into rough or icy waters, he needed a true water dog to fetch it.

So he negotiated with the ship's captain and bought several of the coal-black dogs. Instead of calling them "Newfoundlands," he misnamed them "Labradors." But the "Retriever" in the dog's name fits exactly, for his work in life is to bring back the birds from wherever they fall.

The Earl never ceased to marvel at his new breed. "With a few shakes," he wrote, "the dogs can shed water like oil."

The real miracle of today's Labrador, however, is not his coat but his self-control. A whole flock of ducks can whiz right past his nose, and he will remain steady as a tree stump. Even when the guns fire, and ducks tumble out of the sky, he neither flinches nor pursues. He waits. Then at the command, "Fetch!" he's off like a bullet, crashing through the brush, leaping into the water, heading for the bird.

On windless days he brings it back with lightning speed. But when the wind is high and the tide strong, the fallen bird often drifts out of his sight. Howling for help, he looks ashore, his raised head asking, "Where, Boss? Where?"

"It's over there!" the boss signals with a wave of his arm. To signal after signal the dog responds, until at last he finds the duck bobbing on the water. Then with tender mouth he carries it back to his master.

"For me," one hunter says, "the teamwork between us is the thrill of the sport."

Another hunter, a white-haired veteran, claims that his thrill comes when the bird is delivered so gently that not a feather is ruffled. "What other animal," he asks, "would bring such a tasty morsel to me instead of gobbling it up himself?"

Most Labradors are naturally tender with their birds. For proof, the same old hunter tells a remarkable story. Satin-Soot, a frolicsome pup, was at play one day with two of his litter sisters. Romping in and out of a creek, the sisters were chasing Satin-Soot, who had something in his mouth.

Curious, the old man called the puppy in and took from between his teeth a live baby thrush, whole and unhurt! With words of praise he made this incident the puppy's first lesson in retrieving. Because the Labrador is both gentle and teachable, he is the hunter's fine retriever and everyone's friend.

Boston Terrier—All American

Once upon a time a steamship was plowing along the waters of the Atlantic between Liverpool and Boston. The captain, a stern fellow who disliked dogs, thought that his cargo consisted only of woolens and worsteds. Little did he know that down in the engine room a coal stoker had smuggled aboard a bull-and-terrier dog. This was no ordinary pet; he was a professional fighter!

The stoker knew, of course, that a good fighter would bring good money in Boston. He had sold others there before. But what he never dreamed was that this particular dark-brindled chap would turn out to be the foundation sire of a new American breed.

When the steamer docked, a man named Hooper

bought the stowaway, not because he wanted a prize fighter of a dog but because he liked the dapper look of him—the snow-white bib, the white blaze up his face, the ears cropped, and the screw tail. Here, he thought, was a handsome, bare-fisted fellow with plenty of character. It would be a fine thing to have pups in his image! So he bred the dog, whom he called Judge, to a pure-white Terrier. Sure enough, the pups were not only brindle in color but they took on the character of their sire.

In due time dog fanciers bought up Judge's pups and his grandpups, too. They determined to create a new breed, one that would combine the courage of the Bulldog and the liveliness of the Terrier. This they did. Moreover, the bullishness of the fighter was bred out, and gentleness bred in. The new dog they named the Boston Terrier.

Toby Timmons is the best example I know of this all-American breed. He is no longer alive, but I can still see him gazing up at me, one ear pricked, one flopped over.

Toby was all things to all people. With the youngsters who came to his house he was a boisterous playfellow, jumping and pouncing all over them. To prowlers he was a fierce, growling guardsman.

But with Grandma, a fragile little lady, he was gentleness itself. When she fell one day and broke her hip, he licked her face until she awoke. Then he ran for help.

When Grandma returned home from the hospital, Toby never once dove between her crutches, nor even so much as brushed up against them. Instead, he hovered about her like some diminutive nurse, barking encouragement as she hobbled from room to room.

The only time he left her side was when the ladies of the sewing circle met. The click of shears seemed to fill his small soul with terror, reminding him no doubt of the day his ears were cropped. So always on sewing day Toby slunk off and went fishing.

Patiently he fished the afternoon away. Sometimes perch leaped right at him, surprising him nearly out of his wits. The big ones always got away, but the little ones he caught and fetched home. Then, when the ladies were gone, Grandma rolled the fish in crumbs and fried them for their supper.

In little ways like this, Toby gave Grandma good reason to live on for a long, long time. When at last she died, he soon followed. And these are the words on his grave:

Here lies Toby Timmons—fisherman, friend, and all-around American

The Saint Bernard, Dog of Mercy

BLACK NIGHT OVERTOOK THE LITTLE BAND OF PILGRIMS TOIL-ing their way over the Swiss Alps to Rome. The year was 962, and the mountain pass lay buried in snow.

Suddenly out of the night a pack of robbers waylaid the pilgrims, murdering some, stealing meat and bread from the others.

In panic, the survivors fled to Italy and told their tale of horror to a saintly man named Bernard. He was quiet-faced and mild. Yet there was a terrible courage in him. Before morning he stormed up the mountain with only a handful of men. And when he came upon the bandits, his very fearlessness awed them. He seemed a supreme being, and they fled from his sight.

Bernard was indeed a superior being. When aroused he had the power of an avalanche. Now he was fired with a plan. He would build a shelter for travelers at the summit of the pass.

In time the shelter grew. It was a monastery, bleak on the outside but warm and friendly within. Here laborers crossing the mountain to find work on the other side, or pilgrims going to Rome, or any wayfarer could find comfort and security.

News of the sanctuary spread, and as the years went by more and more travelers braved the pass. Some never reached the shelter house but were lost in snowslides, and some died of cold and exhaustion.

The monks were troubled. If only they could do more! Were dogs the answer? Could the big Swiss hounds be of help? They were descendants of the huge Molossus dogs of Asia and were famous for their scenting powers. Hopefully, the monks knocked at cottage doors in the lowlands, asking, "Would you give us one of your big dogs to run errands of mercy?"

Some of the farmers willingly agreed. And from these Alpine hounds the monks developed a staunch breed, one that could battle the icy world of peaks and crags and eternal snows. Keen of scent, the dogs tracked footsteps even three days old. And when the trail ended in a drift, they pawed the snow away until they found the traveler beneath. Then with warm tongues they licked him awake and led him to the hospice.

For centuries these dogs of mercy went on saving lives. History pictures them with a little wine cask tied about their necks and food strapped to a harness. Always they were enormous fellows with great, kindly faces.

Near the hospice stands a life-size statue of the famous dog, Barry. During his lifetime Barry saved forty victims of snow sleep. Later the dogs were often called "Barry Hounds" in his honor. Only recently were they given the name "Saint Bernard."

Today, with telephone lines going up the Alps and railroads tunneling through, the Saint Bernard has less work to do. But the breed still wears a halo of glory. A new hospice has been built in the high Himalayas, where he is carrying on his mission.

Here in America the Saint Bernard is found in country homes, wherever there is room for a mammoth dog. He romps with the children, and when they are hurt, he gently licks their tears away. By instinct he knows that his role is the comforter.

MUSTARD SEED, THE PET POMERANIAN

NOT EVERYONE CAN RIDE A HIGH-METTLED HORSE. AND not everyone can handle a big, strong dog. Bobby Ann was a teenager who could do both. She had ridden since she was three, and she had owned big dogs—Danes and Dalmatians, even Saint Bernards.

The strange thing about people like Bobby Ann is that you never really know them until their spirit is tested. Just when life stretched out before her with happy, beckoning trails, she was stricken with polio. After the fever burned itself out, she was helpless. Except for one arm.

But now a brave, new Bobby Ann emerged. Of course she had been brave when she took the high jumps on her Thoroughbred. But then it was the horse who had the look of eagles. Now Bobby Ann has it!

With spirit beyond measure she began to plan a new life. She called for paints and an easel; she called for books of adventure. Then, wistfully, she called for pamphlets on dogs. Surely there must be a tiny dog, one easy to lift, yet all that a dog should be.

She studied the toy breeds, and it was the Pomeranian that won

out. He arrived on her birthday, with his kennel name, "Mustard Seed," printed in big letters on his crate.

"We'll keep that name!" Bobby Ann shouted, hugging the ball of fluff close.

"Suits him well," agreed her father. "He's not much bigger than a seed."

"And his coat's the color of mustard blossoms," the mother added.

Bobby Ann was silent. Then, barely lifting her eyes from the dog, she asked, "Do you remember when I was sick?"

She expected no answer and got none.

"Well, one day the minister came and he said to me, 'If ye have faith as a grain of mustard seed, nothing shall be impossible unto you.'" Bobby Ann stroked the wise little face. "And now nothing shall!" She laughed and cried all at the same time.

Mustard Seed is serving his purpose well. He thinks *he* owns Bobby Ann, instead of the other way around. Each morning he fetches his comb and insists upon having his bushy coat groomed. And when things are too quiet, he barks in a high-pitched voice, "Look at me!" Then he turns a string of somersaults—a trick Bobby Ann taught him.

Life to him is busy and full of glee. He growls ferociously at all the delivery men, and he carries notes for Bobby Ann to her mother and proudly brings back the things she requests. All day long he goes around strutting big to make up for his littleness.

Mustard Seed has a heritage to justify his strut. In fact, Bobby Ann painted a picture of his famous ancestors—the great sledge dog of the North and the Wolf-Spitz, who drove cattle in Germany. It was in Germany, in the province of Pomerania, that fanciers bred the Spitz down to toy size.

But in all this evolution the little Pom never lost his resemblance to the big dogs of the Arctic. You can see it in the deep furred coat, in the plume of a tail curled rakishly over his back, in the eager look on his fox-like face.

Verily, he is still the majestic dog of the North—in miniature!

The Great Dane

THIS IS THE STORY OF A GREAT DOG. IT IS FULL OF DANGER and violence, fun and bravery. And it begins centuries ago, in a Roman arena. It is the day of a lion fight. The Romans are surging toward the ring like ants swarming. For this is no ordinary fight between lion and lion. It is a fight between the king of beasts and a dog.

The dog is of great size. His color is one with the lion, and he leaps and runs with leonine swiftness. But the match is uneven, for the lion has four sets of claws, like multiple swords, and his teeth are stilettos.

Yet the Great Dog wins, and the people cry: "He is not dog; he is the god, Vulcan!"

The chief thrill of this story is that it repeats itself. Centuries later, in Germany, the Great Dog is again in combat. This time the odds are almost insuperable. His enemy is the murderous boar, running wild in the Black Forest. Now, instead of charging a lion in an arena, he is the target. And the forest is vast and deep.

A dog's teeth are no match for a boar's tusks. Yet the Great Dog learns to spin and dodge and hold the boar at bay until the hunter rides up with bow and arrow.

With rare skill the Germans trained the Great Dog. They devised a tuskproof vest made of whalebone, and they tied it around the plump bodies of the puppies so they could learn very early the art of dodging the mighty tusks.

By the year 1600, boar hunting became the sport of kings and nobles. German Duke Henry Julius had six hundred boarhounds in his kennel. In one season a hunting party with a pack of hounds actually killed 1,100 boars.

It wasn't very long until the ferocious beast was practically wiped out. Then the Great Dog tackled bear and bison and wolf until at last the Black Forest was safe . . . even for little Red Riding-Hood!

In all these years the Germans developed several strains of the hounds, and each was given a name. The solid-colored hounds were *Ulmers, Bauerhunds,* and *Saupackers.* The *Tiger Dogges* were so called because they were white with black splotches.

But the most common name for all was simply *Deutsche Dogge.*

Then, by a whim of fate, a fawn-colored hound was shipped to Denmark. Her puppies, including a white-and-black-spotted one, were later sent to France. Immediately the French labeled them *Grand Danois,* meaning "Big Danish." The *Tiger Dogge* they called *Harlequin.* And that is how the German names were dropped and the term "Great Dane" came into being.

Noble and dignified as he is, the Great Dane has a delicious sense of what is fun. To him small dogs and cats are fun. He rolls them over as if they were tumbleweeds, and he considers them his pets.

One owner says of her Dane, "My King Haakon is a regal fellow. He scorns toys of any kind, but a pet cat is essential to him. When he looks up from playing with her, he seems to ask: 'Is this so unthinkable? After all, kings do have pets, you know.'

"Then quickly comes my reply: 'But, of course! Of course, kings have pets. It is their divine right!'"

THE TINY PUP FROM CHIHUAHUA

ONCE THERE WAS A WEE SLIP OF AN OPERA SINGER AND her name was Madame Patti. Her singing made so many people happy that they, in turn, wanted to make her happy. Everywhere they lavished gifts upon her. Kings and queens gave her diamonds and pearls. Poor people brought home-baked bread and purple grapes and laid them at her dressing-room door.

But, of all gifts, the midget of Mexico delighted her soul. And this was the way of it:

On a soft, gentle night in Mexico City, when a sickle moon shone in the sky and the wind showered apple blossoms across the grass, the little diva, as they called Madame

Patti, was moved to sing in a kind of triumph—perhaps for the beauty of the night, perhaps for sheer gladness.

Whatever the reason, her joy notes reached out and stirred the listeners, too, and one among them left the opera hall and gathered together the loveliest bouquet he could find. In the center of it he tucked a memento from Mexico—a Chihuahua dog, the tiniest breed in the whole world. It was a delicate fawn color, and so tiny that its legs were scarce bigger than flower stems and its head no larger than a blossom.

With the dog still held fast among the flowers, the man arrived back at the opera hall in time to hear the grand finale of *The Barber of Seville*. He watched the whole audience rise with huzzahs and handclappings to pay homage to Madame Patti, and he waited while the curtain had to be rung up to the sum of five times.

When the clamoring finally ceased and the flutes and violins had played their last notes, a great stillness fell over the hall as the man with the bouquet marched down the aisle.

Madame Patti stepped in front of the curtain and impulsively gathered the flowers to her. Just as she brought them to her face, a piquant little head peered out and a pair of dark eyes studied her with a droll and saucy expression. How she laughed and laughed, while the audience stamped and cheered, and the bewildered pup cocked his head from side to side.

Now in the bright circle of light the two diminutive creatures welcomed each other, one with a quick curling of his tongue, the other with kisses and soft murmurings.

At last Madame Patti lifted the Chihuahua out from the bouquet and said, "Dear friends! From each country I like to take with me a token of remembrance, but never before"—and here her eyes sparkled—"no, never have I been given a live one. *Butterfly* I shall call him, for his ears flare out exactly like butterfly wings. No?" she asked with a lifting of her brows.

"*Si! Si!*" the audience cried in rapture. Here was a fairy tale come true! Their own native dog from the state of Chihuahua going home with the little diva whom they adored!

And when, for her encore, she sang *Home, Sweet, Sweet Home,* the Chihuahua's eyes grew big and luminous as if already he knew that he had found home.

HERR DOBERMANN'S PINSCHER

SOME SIXTY-ODD YEARS AGO, IN THE CITY OF APOLDA, Germany, there lived a man with derring-do. His name was Herr Louis Dobermann, and he had a dream. He longed to create the most perfect species of dog in the whole world.

Why couldn't he do it, he asked his two best friends, the grave digger and the bell ringer.

The men shrugged and repeated the question. Why couldn't he? Was not Herr Louis the town's dog-catcher? Did he not have all manner of dogs to work with?

He did, indeed, but that made his task of selection all the harder. What he really had in mind was to produce a "sharp" dog, and by "sharp" he meant a dog that would attack as quickly as a struck match bursts into flame. For the city of Apolda was rich in factories and warehouses and fine homes, and their owners wanted day-and-night protection from thieves. They were continually asking Herr Louis for good watchdogs.

So one day he put on his thinking cap and began to plan, exactly like some chef concocting a new dish. For his perfect dog he needed swiftness and agility, which Terriers could provide. And he needed the keen mind of the German Shepherd, and the strength of the big dog known as the Butcher's Dog. But could all these traits be blended?

As luck would have it, he had recently caught in his net one of  the lively Terriers known as "Pinschers." Her name was Schnupp, and if she were mated with bigger dogs, her offspring might well be giant Pinschers—not clumsy at all, but lithe.

Herr Dobermann's dream did not come true in a flash. Schnupp did become the matriarch of the new breed, but it was many, many generations before the great Doberman Pinscher emerged as we know him.

Today the Doberman is young as breeds go, but he is most distinctive and distinguished. He is the lean aristocrat, tall and well proportioned. His coat is short and hard, and lies so close to the skin it looks as if some master tailor had just turned him out. Generally this coat is black as polished ebony, with tan markings for emphasis. His tail is docked very short, and his ears are cropped and set high in erect points. This makes him look always ready to take off.

Nimble as a gazelle, he can run with the same speed. In every galloping stride his hind legs actually leap ahead of his forelegs! It is a handsome sight to see him flash in and out of a hedge, like some black needle in the sun.

Fierce he can be, but only when he is trained and then ordered to attack. He is too much the gentleman-detective to bite people promiscuously. "Watchdog supreme" is his title, and he wears it with dignity.

In factories and big stores he and the night watchman are ever on the alert. Guns can't hear and they can't smell, and sometimes they jam and don't go off. But Herr Dobermann's Pinscher is sure-fire.

Yet with all his quick trigger action, he is a thinker, too, not a killer—except on command. The sharpness that Herr Louis wanted is there, and with it a high fidelity for his job, even unto death.

LITTLE DIE-HARD, THE SCOT'S TERRIER

H E HAILS FROM THE WINDY MOORS OF SCOTLAND, THIS rough-haired fellow with the jaw that says do-or-die. He has a single purpose in life—to "go to earth" and drag foxes and rats from their holes. Nature built him short-legged for his underground work, with feet strong and tough for digging. And she grizzled his coat so that in heather or hedgerow his busyness would be unnoticed.

"Earth dogges" is the way King James VI described his own Scotch Terriers. He was a learned man and liked to explain that the very name "Terrier" came from the Latin word *terra*, meaning "earth."

This young King of Scotland was a clever one

with dogs, and a clever one with talk. When he entertained royalty from countries known for their big dogs, he always managed to get in a word about his own wee Scotties.

"Gude gear comes in bittic bundles," he would chuckle. "'Tis an old Highland saying, that, and it fits our towsy tykes the way a ring fits its finger."

The world over, the Scotch Terrier answers to names like Tousle or Whiskers. In fact, the more whiskers he grows, the better he is liked. Chin whiskers add greatly to his determined look, and two clumps of bushy brows make his shoe-button eyes gleam like black diamonds. For practical purposes the heavy brows are watersheds in case of rain, and mudguards when he is tunneling. His whole body is covered with bristles so that his enemies can never get a good hold on him. To them he is a slithery fellow, most exasperating!

For exhibitions Scotties are often trimmed and plucked so that their underwear shows. This is soft as lamb's wool. But a working Terrier is never plucked, for then rats and foxes with their needle-like teeth might tear him to pieces. His teeth, by the way, are as wondrous as his coat. They are extremely strong and large, larger even than a Collie's! As for his heart, it is game and fearless. He always faces the battle with stubborn courage, a trait which has earned him the title of Little Die-Hard.

Has all this talk of fighting misled you? The Scotch Terrier is not only a fighter. He can be the most dependable baby sitter, alert and wide-awake until relieved of his duty. One Scottie I know will let the baby play with enticing squeak toys—rabbits and mice and teddy bears—and though the noises set him a-quiver, he never snatches the toys away. He just looks on, old and wise in the ways of babies.

Some people feel that Scotties are born old. From the time they are puppies they seem solemn and dignified. Perhaps it is the beetling brows and square jaws which make them look like sober businessmen. What if their business *is* rats? Is not the work of the exterminator a praiseworthy occupation?

King James thought so. He was exceedingly proud of his dog, Jowler, who was, of course, a great ratter. Jowler had the entire run of the castle, including the banquet halls. Yet the King, holding both his sides in laughter, would taunt his chief cook, "Listen, mon! Jowler prefers my stable to your table!"

THE ARCTIC SLED DOGS

A TEAM OF HUSKIES STANDS HOWLING IN HARNESS. IT IS the year 1925, late January. The place is Nenana, a bleak Alaskan village.

The driver is working fast, loading a small package on the sled, wrapping it in furs. If he does not take the handlebars soon, the dogs will begin chewing at their harness. They are wild to go! It is as if they knew the package contains life-saving serum to be rushed to Nome. An epidemic of diphtheria is raging, and only the serum can halt it.

Over at the airstrip the plane scheduled to carry the package is grounded by storms. But weather is no barrier to the Arctic sled dogs. At the command "Mush!" they're off, streaking across the snow, jumping over ice hummocks, galloping for the sheer fun of it.

Along the trail other teams stand ready. At Shaktolik, the famous racer Seppalla waits with his lead dog Togo and a team of twenty. Seppalla has a message from Nome: DON'T CUT ACROSS NORTON BAY. HURRICANE WINDS BREAKING UP ICE. But Seppalla pays no heed. Going around would mean hours! He cracks his whip, shouts, "Let's go!"

Across the glare ice Togo feels his way. He knows this short cut well, but today the ice is buckling, splinters are tearing loose, ripping the pads of his feet. With paws bleeding he and his teammates finish the sixty-mile lap, howling not in pain, but in jealousy that a new relay is taking over.

Night comes. And morning. And night again. Team after team carries the precious cargo. The wind grows angrier—sixty miles an hour, then eighty! The temperature falls to fifty below. Gunnar Kasson is the new driver with big black Balto his leader.

But let Gunnar tell his own story.

"I took the serum at Bluff. The snow was raging. I hitched the dogs. I wanted to get to Point Safety before the trails got impassable.

"I stuck to the coast, figuring it would be good going. The wind was howling in from the north, picking up the snow like it was a comb. I didn't know

where I was. But Balto sniffed the trail through the snow and kept pushing ahead.

"The sled spilled over, and I had to untangle the dogs' harness and lift the stuff back and get going again. It was black night. When we got to Point Safety I mushed by the roadhouse. Everything was dark. Balto and the others were going good now. I decided to go on instead of waking the next driver for the last twenty miles.

"By now the snow had drifted and the air was stinging cold. Two dogs began to stiffen up. I made a rabbit-skin covering for them, but the cold went through it. Somehow, at 5:36 on the morning of February second, we staggered into Nome."

A wildly cheering huddle of humanity greeted Gunnar Kasson. But he did not hear. His arms were around Balto and he was half crying as he rubbed the dog's legs.

Today, in Central Park, New York, a large statue of a Husky commemorates the thrilling race. The inscription on it reads:

Dedicated to the indomitable spirit of the sled dogs that relayed antitoxin 600 miles over rough ice, through Arctic blizzards, from Nenana to the relief of stricken Nome.

Some say the statue is of Balto, and some say, "No! It is Togo, or Fox, or Scotty." But what does it matter? Even Gunnar Kasson or Seppalla would say, "It fits them all!"

The Dachshund—Big Enough

PANIC CAME OVER ME. I DID NOT WANT A LITTLE DOG. I WANTED a great, big dog—one to sprawl by the fire, one so big that I could sit on the floor and rest my heavy riding boots on his belly without hurting him in the least.

But the telegram trembling in my hand said: AM SENDING YOU A DACHSHUND PUP. UNLESS YOU WIRE WILL SHIP TOMORROW. HE'LL ARRIVE MID-NIGHT CHICAGO AIRPORT. DON'T WORRY IF PUP IS AIRSICK. WON'T HURT HIM AT ALL. HIS KENNEL NAME IS JANDELO'S ALEX.

A Dachshund pup! I could see him now. A caricature of a dog, an animated sausage! I read the telegram again. UNLESS YOU WIRE . . . The phone was at my elbow. Ten little words would keep him away. Just pick up the receiver. Do it!

But I seemed under a spell. In my mind I already saw the crate, with the frightened eyes looking out, and the pup not really airsick, just bewildered and lonely for his litter brothers and sisters.

When Alex arrived, he was not bewildered at all. With wagging tail he strutted out of the crate—a gnomelike little fellow, except for his proud chest, which stuck out like a prize fighter's.

For good reason we had called our place Mole Meadow. But, even as a pup, Alex declared war on the moles. Yapping and barking in excitement, he found their winding runs. Then making a ditch digger of himself, he shoveled the dirt away with his forepaws. As for his nose, it pushed on ahead, like some pointed plow, until it came upon the culprit.

Mole Meadow is a misnomer now. We haven't seen one in so long that I've forgotten what they look like. No, I'll take that back. I do remember. They have softly padded feet with hard claws for digging, just like Alex. And they have a pointed muzzle—like his, too. But there the resemblance ends. He is all merry light-heartedness, and they are dark and drab as the tunnels they burrow.

In ridding our place of moles and mice and woodchucks and rabbits, Alex is living up to his inheritance. His family tree goes back to the fifteenth century, to the badger hounds who were bred by the foresters of Germany.

In German, *dachs* means "badger" and *hund* means "dog." Hence the name of this courageous little hunter who is built long and low for the special purpose of burrowing into badgers' holes.

In spite of their short legs, Dachshunds can leap and bound and run fast enough to follow the trail of a horse or a deer. Always when I go riding, Alex trots along, tracking our scent even when we gallop out of sight.

On fall nights, after a brisk hour across country, he likes to toast his bones by the fire. As for me, nothing is so nice as to pull off my boots and wriggle my toes under his warm body. Too small? No, indeed. He's just the right size!

MANY PUREBREDS MAKE THE MONGREL

AT THE EDGE OF A SWAMP TOUCHING THE WATERS OF Green Bay, Wisconsin, there is a warm and cozy dog pound where pups without pedigrees are welcome as jonquils in spring.

It was not always so. Once, the old gray building was a shambles. Snow and wind and rain blew in through the cracks. Once, it housed but a handful of orphaned pups and bedraggled strays. Night and day they howled their misery. It was as if they knew that just across the road a great black furnace stood waiting to eat them up; that is, if they were not adopted.

The boy, Larry, who lived nearby,

hated the furnace. On his way to fish in the marsh he hurried past it, scarce breathing, scarce looking. To him it was an evil monster, licking its chops, awaiting its prey.

But some days, without his willing it, Larry's eye was drawn to the wide, jawlike door and to the red licks of fire showing through the airholes. On those days his fishing spree was only half fun, for as he fished he watched the wild birds flying free, and he heard the prisoners crying in the pound. Then he gathered up his own dog, hugging him close.

The black furnace worried Larry, and at night he dreamed about the caged-up dogs. Always in his dream he strode into the pound in seven-league boots. Quickly pulling one off, he filled it to overflowing with dogs, dogs, dogs. Then he spirited them away to Never-Never Land, where eager children claimed them all.

One bleak November day Larry's dream practically came true. His father was appointed master of the pound! Suddenly a whole new world opened out for Larry. He was no longer a boy who just fished and played in the swamp. He became man-grown overnight.

There was so much to do! The dogs needed help quickly. One had a rasping cough; one, a mere pup, wheezed like some old man. And the others were so poor and starved that Larry's father shook his fist at the owners who had deserted them. "Heartless idiots!" he spoke in a rage. "*They* be the curs, not these helpless ones!"

The boy, listening, felt a surge of pride in his father. "Pa," he said, "even if no one claims them, we don't *have* to put them to death; do we, Pa?"

The father set his lips in a line. "That we don't! To my way, every dog is entitled to a home. We'll cure their ills and fatten 'em up. Then you'll see! Somebody will want them."

With a fierce crusading spirit, man and boy went to work. They scrubbed and scoured the cages. They stuffed gunny sacks around the window frames. They built a fire in the old pot-bellied stove and put kettles of water on top to boil. The steam filled every corner of the room, and the pup with the wheeze began to breathe quietly. As for the dog with the cough, he made a furry ball of himself and soon dropped off to sleep.

Every morning now Larry was up before daylight—stirring a big batch of gruel, filling the water pans, feeding the dogs, and then letting them out of their cages to romp in the big room. This play period was his own idea. "If children need a recess," he argued with himself, "why don't animals?"

But one little moppet was a problem dog. She refused to come out and play. She refused even to eat. Whenever food was offered, her lip curled up over her fangs and the growl in her throat was deep and menacing.

Larry did not laugh at the big noise coming from so small a creature. He felt a kind of hurt that anyone could mistrust him. He named the unfriendly pup "Muggs" and determined to win her for a pet.

For days he brought her choice morsels from his own plate. For days he talked softly to her whenever he went by her cage. "Oh, you're the ugly one," he would say, his voice gentle with reproof. "But we're going to change that. You've got Terrier blood, which shows you're smart. And you've got a Bulldog jaw for spunk. Why, you've got lots of purebred blood. Anyone can see that!"

One evening after school Larry brought Muggs a pair of toy mice, and for a long time she held them in her mouth, with only the tails sticking out. Who could growl with a mouthful of mice? Not Muggs.

It was months, though, before she ventured out of her cage at recess. When at last she did, she found it such fun that she didn't want to go back. Cunningly, she figured a way to make the time last longer. When the hour of play was up, she ran to the pan of drinking water. But her tongue barely touched it. She wasn't drinking at all, just pretending so that Larry would

swoop her up and carry her to the cage like some helpless child. Shyly at first, she dabbed at his cheek with her tongue; then her tail did a little tattoo against his ribs.

"You rascal!" he laughed at her. "You were just stalling."

There was a kind of magic in the way Muggs blossomed. She soon became a "trusty" with all manner of special privileges.

Now when Larry makes his rounds of the restaurants to collect scraps, Muggs leaps onto his bicycle and goes along. Balancing herself on the handlebars, she likes to let the wind stream past her face. It tickles her nose with the scent of the huge joints of beef in the basket. But never will she touch one until Larry gives the signal.

Today Muggs is the pet of the pound, smart and obedient as any circus dog. She climbs ladders. She dances like a ballerina. She jumps through hoops. And she will perch for long minutes on the rooftree of her house until told to come down.

But the magic does not end with Muggs. The whole pound has been transformed! Now when the wind howls around the gray building, the big room is a friendly place—the teakettles singing, the father's pencil scratching at his reports, the boy building new kennels, and the dogs snoozing or just listening to the radio.

To Larry's great delight the cages are filling up. Instead of just a handful of dogs, there are dozens. Some days the phone rings again and again:

"Come get a mangy mutt running loose on Shawano Avenue."

"Come get a slinking cur hanging around my meat market."

"Come get a mother dog and her assorted pups from under our porch."

All these are made welcome at the pound. Even the runtiest.

*Some*body will want him, Larry and his father insist. And some-body always does. Half-pint, an undersized pup, lived a whole year at the pound before someone recognized the goodness in his homely little face and tucked him into a child's Christmas stock-ing. In his adopted home Half-pint soon lost his sad-eyed look and became an active partner in raising a small child.

Larry's father is very firm in this matter of adoption. Always he follows up to see that the dog is happy. And if the dog is mistreated, he is promptly brought back. Then there is such a tail-wagging of joy that the returning fellow is apt to become another of Larry's personal pets. "We need some old-timers, don't we, Pa, to help train the new and frightened ones?"

And the father smiles, secretly happy because the boy understands. "You're right, Larry. Each life—man or dog—has a pur-pose in this big old world. Here we've got herders and hunters, burrowers and retriev-ers, and just plain foot warmers."

"Yes, Pa. Everything but pedigreed dogs."

The father's eye fondles the dogs in the nearest cages. "Remember, son, it takes many purebreds to make a mongrel. And each mongrel is the only one of its kind. That's why I like 'em."

"Me, too, Pa."

"Does the Red Cross worry about the ancestry of its dogs? Does the Army Medical Corps? Do circus trainers? . . . No!" the father barks, sounding for all the world like one of his own dogs. Then his voice quiets. "After all, mongrels with their mixed-up backgrounds are good Americans. Loyal, that's what they are, and anxious to please. You know that!"

"Sure!" agrees Larry.

And there, in happy proof, is Muggs looking up at him with love and with asking eyes: "Shall I climb the ladder? Jump through the hoop? What will it be? Just you name it, Larry."

For their help the author and artist
are grateful to:

A. D. ALEXANDER, *secretary*
Collie Club of America, Inc.

MRS. NATHAN R. ALLEN, *president*
Poodle Club of America

MISS EMMELINE ANDRUSKEVICZ, adviser

MRS. L. W. BONNEY, *secretary*
Dalmatian Club of America

WILLIAM F. BROWN, *editor*
The American Field

HOWES BURTON, *secretary*
Labrador Retriever Club, Inc.

ACKNOWLEDGMENTS

MRS. L. E. CAFFALL, *chairman of Information and Publicity*

Poodle Club of America

I. W. CARREL, *editor*

Hounds and Hunting

MISS FRANCES J. CARTER

Pomeranian and Pekingese fancier

MRS. WALTER P. CHRYSLER

Chihuahua fancier

MISS BARBARA CORY

Pomeranian fancier

MRS. JOHN W. CROSS, JR., *secretary*

Dachshund Club of America

MRS. NICHOLAS A. DEMIDOFF

Husky breeder and racer

Monadnock Kennels

ACKNOWLEDGMENTS

MAJOR CLARK DENNY

United States Air Force

RUDY DOCKY, clown

Pollack Brothers Shrine Circus

RALPH B. HENRY, mentor

GEORGE M. HOWARD, *president*

American Boxer Club, Inc.

C. K. HUNTER, *secretary*

English Springer Spaniel Club of the Central States

ROBERT CAPRON HUNTER, JR.

Springer Spaniel fancier

MRS. DOROTHY E. HUSTED, *secretary*

American Pomeranian Club, Inc.

REV. RUSSELL E. KAUFFMAN, *first vice-president*

The Chihuahua Club of America

ACKNOWLEDGMENTS

MISS MILDRED G. LATHROP, reference librarian

E. PERKINS MCGUIRE, *secretary*
American Boxer Club, Inc.

EUGENE J. RIORDAN, *secretary*
Boston Terrier Club of America, Inc.

MRS. EDNA R. SECOR, *secretary*
Bulldog Club of America

CURTICE W. SLOAN, *president*
Doberman Pinscher Club of America

WILLIAM I. SHEARER III, *secretary*
Siberian Husky Club of America

MISS MAUREEN SMITH Maur-Ray
German Shepherd Kennels

MRS. GRANT L. SUTTON, adviser

ACKNOWLEDGMENTS

CLARENCE and LARRY VERHEYDEN

Mongrel fanciers

MRS. EARL VOGT

Scotch Terrier fancier

LESTER E. WALLACK

American Spaniel Club

ANTHONY WELLING

Cleveland Mounted Police

MISS IDA G. WILSON, librarian

For the "Naughty Chair" incident we are indebted
to Miss Violet Stefanich and to the publica-
tion, *Our Dumb Animals.*